W9-BDG-399

LANDMARKS OF DEMOCRACY
AMERICAN INSTITUTIONS

THE U.S. POSTAL SERVICE

THE HISTORY OF AMERICA'S MAIL SYSTEM

MARGARET UPHALL

PowerKiDS
press
New York

Clifton Park - Halfmoon Public Library
475 Moe Road
Clifton Park, New York 12065

Published in 2018 by The Rosen Publishing Group, Inc.
29 East 21st Street, New York, NY 10010

Copyright © 2018 by The Rosen Publishing Group, Inc.

All rights reserved. No part of this book may be reproduced in any form without permission in writing from the publisher, except by a reviewer.

First Edition

Editor: Elizabeth Krajnik
Book Design: Reann Nye

Photo Credits: Cover B Christopher/Alamy.com; p. 5 Richard Cavalleri/Shutterstock.com; p. 6 https://commons.wikimedia.org/wiki/File:Articles_page1.jpg; p. 7 Courtesy of the New York Public Library; p. 9 Robert Holmes/Corbis Documentary/Getty Images; p. 11 Science & Society Picture Library/SSPL/Getty Images; p. 12 https://commons.wikimedia.org/wiki/File:Postmarks_Pony_Express.jpg; p. 13 https://commons.wikimedia.org/wiki/File:Owney_with_tags.jpg; p. 14 https://commons.wikimedia.org/wiki/File:Montgomery_Blair,_photo_three-quarters_length_seated.jpg; p. 15 https://commons.wikimedia.org/wiki/File:JHRegan.jpg; pp. 16, 19 Courtesy of the Library of Congress; p. 17 Everett Historical/Shutterstock.com; p. 18 Hulton Deutsch/Corbis Historical/Getty Images; p. 20 https://commons.wikimedia.org/wiki/File:De_Havilland_Airmail_Plane_-299_(2535935153).jpg; p. 21 Underwood Archives/Archive Photos/Getty Images; p. 22 https://commons.wikimedia.org/wiki/File:Uspsheadquartersatlenfantplaza.jpg.

Cataloging-in-Publication Data

Names: Uphall, Margaret.
Title: The U.S. Postal Service: The History of America's Mail System / Margaret Uphall.
Description: New York : PowerKids Press, 2018. | Series: Landmarks of democracy: American institutions | Includes index.
Identifiers: ISBN 9781508161059 (pbk.) | ISBN 9781508161073 (library bound) | ISBN 9781508161066 (6 pack)
Subjects: LCSH: United States Postal Service-Juvenile literature. | Postal service-United States-Juvenile literature.
Classification: LCC HE6371.U64 2018 | DDC 383'.4973-dc23

7549

Manufactured in the United States of America

CPSIA Compliance Information: Batch #BS17PK: For Further Information contact Rosen Publishing, New York, New York at 1-800-237-9932

CONTENTS

COLONIAL POSTAL SERVICE

Today, many people think of the postal service as "snail mail," meaning it takes longer to receive actual mail than an e-mail or a text message. Although this may be true, the U.S. Postal Service plays a very important role in keeping the country—and the world—connected.

During the early years of the British colonies in North America, there wasn't a true postal service. Many people who wished to send mail had to ask their friends—or often a complete stranger, such as a merchant—to deliver it. In 1639, colonial leaders started creating post offices in **taverns** and other locations.

PRESENT-DAY **BOSTON, MASSACHUSETTS**

The first post office in the British colonies in North America was the Fairbanks Tavern in Boston, Massachusetts.

THE CONSTITUTIONAL POST

In 1753, King George II appointed Benjamin Franklin and William Hunter as co-postmasters general of the colonies. However, in 1774, Franklin was removed from his position because he sided with the colonies against Great Britain. In the months before the American **Revolution**, mail was often **intercepted** by the British and used to accuse colonists of **treason**.

Go all to whom

INSTITUTION INSIGHT

The Articles of Confederation, the first U.S. constitution, gave Congress the power to create post offices and postal routes. In 1789, the Constitution created the federal post office and the Office of the Postmaster General.

Goddard's plan for the Constitutional Post laid the foundation for the U.S. Postal Service. Goddard was appointed to the position of surveyor of the post.

William Goddard had the idea to create the Constitutional Post to make sure that colonists received important information regarding the revolutionary cause. The Second Continental Congress authorized Goddard's plan and appointed Benjamin Franklin as postmaster general on July 26, 1775.

THE RISE OF THE STAGECOACH

After the American Revolution ended, the United States began to **expand** westward. This called for additional postal services to carry mail over greater distances. In 1785, Congress authorized **stagecoach** companies to carry mail from one post office to another on certain routes.

Stagecoaches allowed post carriers to deliver a larger volume of mail at one time. However, Postmaster General Ebenezer Hazard started using mail riders on some routes to cut costs because stagecoaches were more expensive. President George Washington did not approve of Hazard's decision because he thought stagecoaches had more advantages. Stagecoaches carried passengers, but carrying the mail as well allowed stagecoach companies to make a **profit**.

Stagecoaches were very uncomfortable to ride in. In 1828, Lewis Downing and Stephen Abbot created the Concord coach, a more comfortable stagecoach.

NEW DELIVERY METHODS

As the United States continued to expand westward, new methods of carrying both people and mail appeared. The steam engine **revolutionized** mail delivery. Starting in 1811, steamboats began to carry mail along U.S. rivers and other waterways. The people who operated these boats had to follow certain rules about mail delivery and played a very important role in the success of the postal service.

Delivering mail by boat wasn't always the fastest method. Mail sent from New York to California would often take more than a month to arrive. Sending mail overland also took a long time. A faster way was needed.

INSTITUTION INSIGHT

The mail delivery route from New York to California had many steps. First, mail would be shipped to Panama by boat. Then, people carried the mail across Panama by canoe or mule. From there, the mail was placed on another boat and shipped to San Francisco.

The *New Orleans* made the first steamboat trip on the Mississippi River. It left Pittsburgh, Pennsylvania, on October 20, 1811, and reached New Orleans, Louisiana, in January 1812.

The Pony Express was an overland mail delivery system started in April 1860. It was created to deliver mail quicker. In some areas, delivery time was cut in half. A post rider carried the mail from one station to the next, where he would change horses. These stations were usually 10 to 15 miles (16.1 to 24.1 km) apart. A rider could cover 75 to 100 miles (120.7 to 160.9 km) each day. The Pony Express ran between Saint Joseph, Missouri, and Sacramento, California— almost 2,000 miles.

The Pony Express only lasted about 18 months. The growing popularity of the railroad and the completion of a cross-country **telegraph** line ended the service in October 1861.

PONY EXPRESS POSTMARKS

📍 INSTITUTION INSIGHT

The Railway Mail Service had its own **mascot**—Owney the dog. Owney followed mailbags across New York, the country, and even the world! The postal workers in Albany, New York, saved the tags people put on him during his travels.

Railway mail delivery began in 1832. Starting in 1862, clerks sorted the mail between stops. This service allowed people living in **rural** areas to have their mail delivered quicker than ever before.

MAIL DELIVERY IN CITIES

When mail services began in the United States, mail was delivered to the post office, where people would go and pick it up.

GENERAL MONTGOMERY BLAIR

When Postmaster General Montgomery Blair cut off mail service to the Confederate States of America in 1861, they had to create their own postal service. John H. Reagan was the only Confederate postmaster general.

Mail carriers used to work between 9 and 12 hours a day Monday through Saturday. They also worked parts of Sunday if necessary. In 1888, Congress passed a law giving letter carriers an eight-hour workday.

JOHN H. REAGAN

Free city delivery to homes and businesses was created as a response to the long lines of people waiting to receive word from Civil War soldiers. Joseph Briggs, a postal worker from Cleveland, Ohio, suggested the idea to Postmaster General Montgomery Blair. Blair took the idea of free city delivery to Congress. Beginning July 1, 1863, mail delivery was free in certain cities throughout the United States. After the war ended, the Postal Service employed many Civil War veterans as letter carriers.

RURAL FREE DELIVERY

Although cities in America continued to grow throughout the late 19th century, many Americans still lived in rural areas. This prevented them from having their mail delivered to their homes. It was also difficult for many of these people to go into a city to get their mail.

Some of the rural free delivery service's largest supporters were the National Grange, National Farmers' Congress, and State Farmers' Alliance. However, in order for the service to be successful, rural customers had to support it.

JOHN WANAMAKER

Postmaster General John Wanamaker suggested rural free delivery to help farmers and their families feel less **isolated**. In 1890, Congress set aside $10,000 ($255,535 in today's currency) to test Wanamaker's rural free delivery plan. After many years of experimenting, different plans, and more funding, a rural free delivery service became permanent on July 1, 1902.

DEVELOPMENTS IN THE 20TH CENTURY

The 20th century involved many changes not only for the United States as a whole, but for its postal system. The Postal Service changed what items could be delivered, putting a parcel post system into place on January 1, 1913. This allowed people to have larger items delivered to their homes.

People living in rural areas were the ones who needed a parcel post system the most. It made deliveries less expensive for rural Americans and made them feel less isolated.

POSTAL SAVINGS FUND VAULT

Another new service was the postal savings system. Starting in 1911, people could **deposit** their money at certain post offices just as they could at a bank. This system was popular until after World War II, when banks provided people with better benefits. The postal savings system officially ended on July 1, 1967.

revolutionized the speed at which Americans received their mail. The first scheduled airmail route, which ran between New York and Washington, D.C., began on May 15, 1918. Soon, plans for an airmail route from New York to San Francisco, California, were put into place. One by one, parts of this route were added.

INSTITUTION INSIGHT

Early airmail was only flown by day because the aircraft of the time didn't have radios or tools to find their way after dark. At night, trains carried the mail. It wasn't until February 22, 1921, that mail was flown from New York to San Francisco overnight.

While most people sent regular letters and packages via airmail, sometimes they sent even more precious cargo. This woman was sent via airmail to San Diego, California, in 1919.

Zip codes were introduced in 1943 in larger cities because many postal workers were entering the armed forces. With many new employees, the Postal Service wanted to make the mail sorting system simpler. Under this system, locations were identified by numbers. The Postal Service started using zip codes nationwide on July 1, 1963.

MODERN MAIL

In the 21st century, the U.S. Postal Service has changed to deal with changing times and communication trends. Many businesses today allow their customers to pay their bills without receiving a paper bill in the mail, which affects the Postal Service. There has been a great decrease in the amount of mail that is sent every day. In 2015, the Postal Service delivered 58.9 billion fewer pieces of mail than it did in 2006.

In 2017, the House of Representatives introduced the Postal Service Reform Act of 2017. This act aims to provide taxpayers with more affordable mailing costs and other benefits to keep the Postal Service modern.

POST OFFICE HEADQUARTERS, WASHINGTON, D.C.

GLOSSARY

deposit: To put something away for safety in a bank or a similar place.

expand: To become bigger.

intercept: To take, seize, or stop something before it reaches where it's supposed to go.

isolated: Separate from others.

mascot: Something, such as an animal or person, seen to represent a group or organization; sometimes thought to bring good luck.

profit: The amount of money made after all expenses are taken out.

revolution: A movement to overthrow an established government.

revolutionize: To change greatly or completely.

rural: Relating to the country.

stagecoach: A large carriage pulled by horses that was used in the past to carry passengers and mail along a regular route.

tavern: A place where people eat and drink.

telegraph: A system of sending messages over long distances by using wires and electrical signals.

treason: The act of trying to overthrow a government.

INDEX

WEBSITES

Due to the changing nature of Internet links, PowerKids Press has developed an online list of websites related to the subject of this book. This site is updated regularly. Please use this link to access the list: www.powerkidslinks.com/lod/mail